# SUMMER

## write and draw journal

**Belongs To:**

Name: ______________________

Grade: ______________________

CAR